THIS BOOK BELONGS TO:

Copyright © 2023

All rights reserved.

No part of this publication may be reproduced, distributed, or transmitted in any form or by any means, including photocopying, recording, or other electronic or mechanical methods, without the prior written permission of the publisher, except in the case of brief quotations embodied in critical reviews and certain other noncommercial uses permitted by copyright law. For permission requests, write to the publisher.

I can
do this

Keep
going!

Stay
hydrated!

I am
loved

I AM
DOING
MY BEST

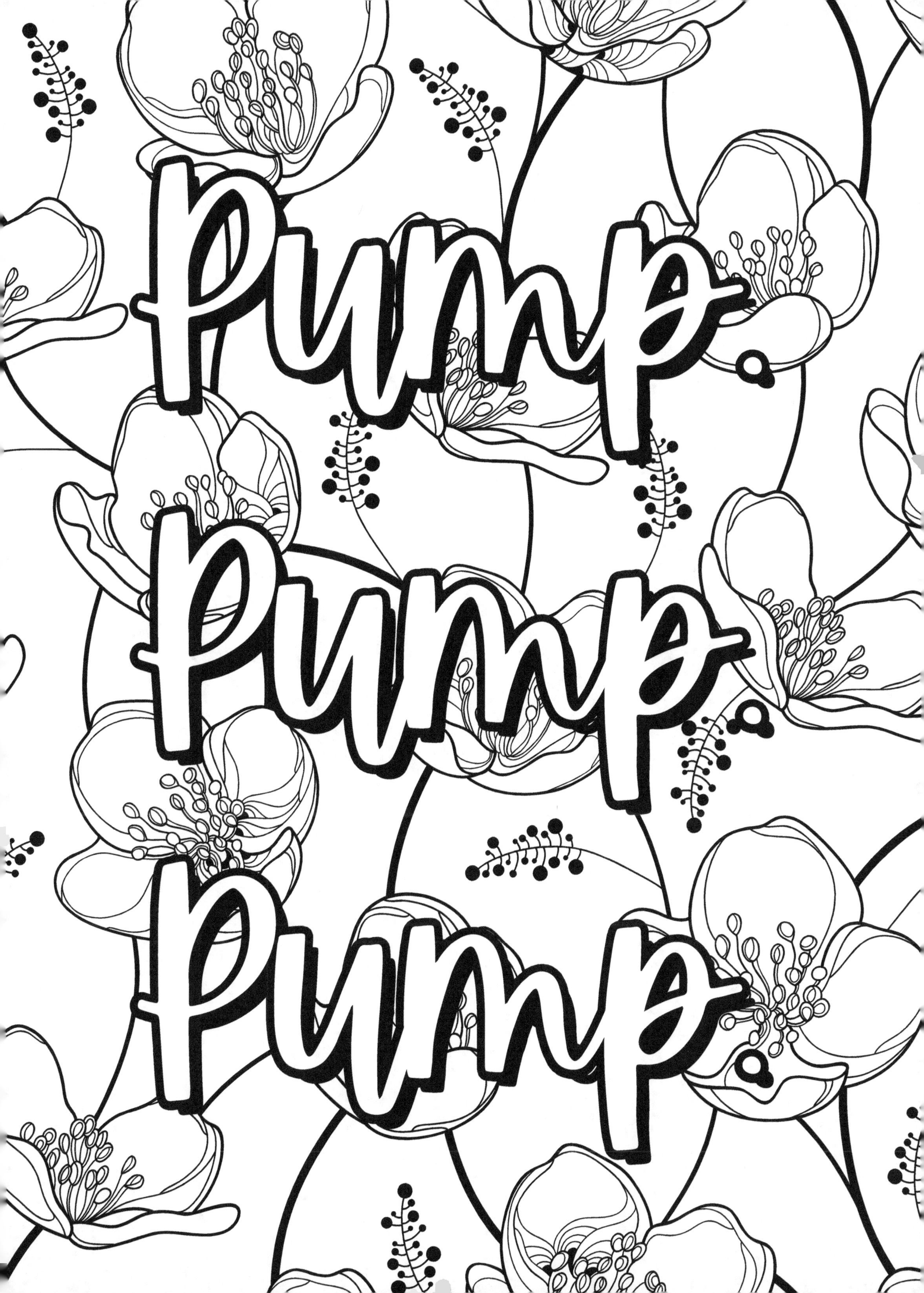

Pump
Pump
Pump

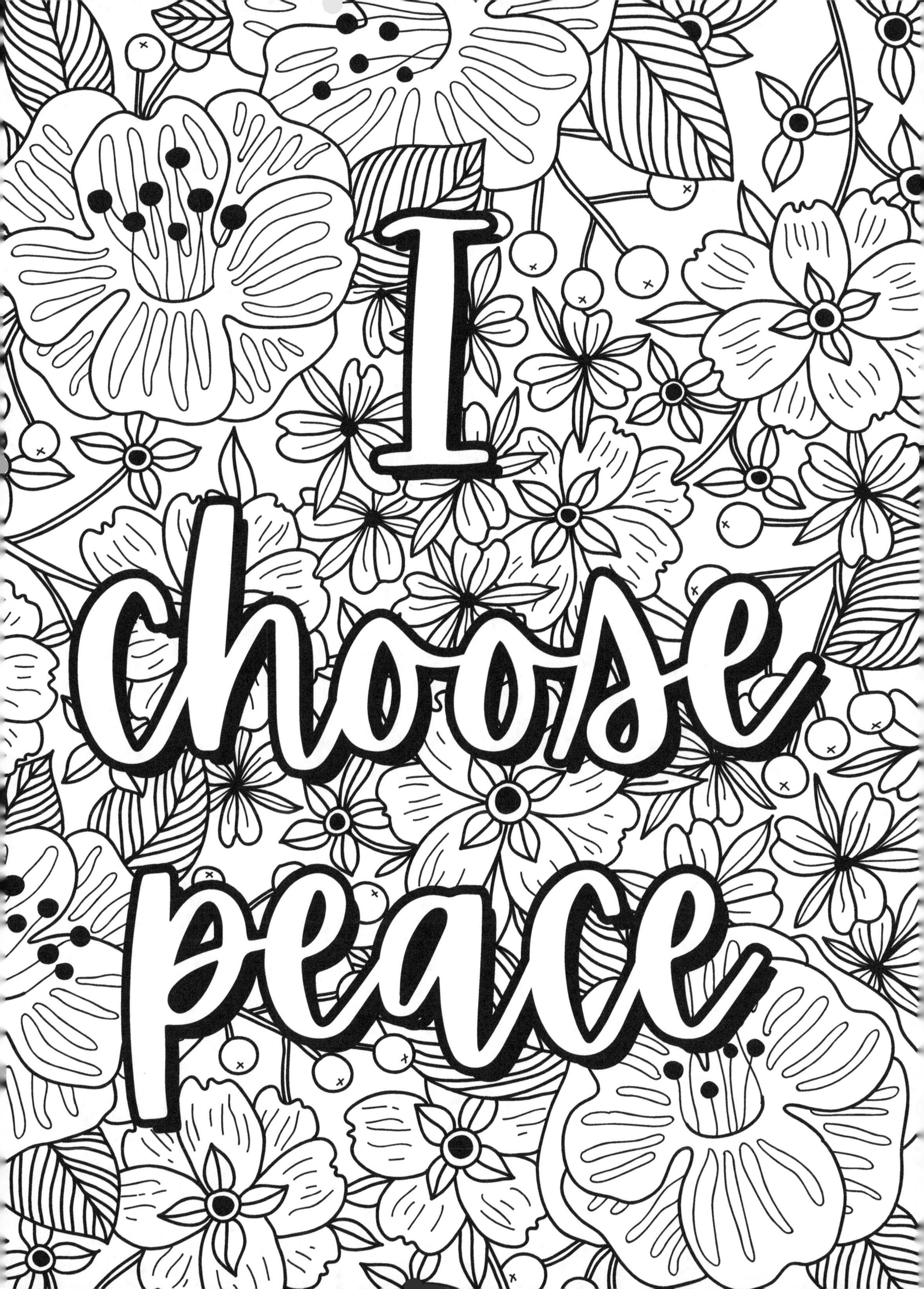

I
choose
peace

I am
important

I am
amazing

Grateful

I matter

I love
myself

I am
proud of
myself

I choose
happiness

I am
beautiful

www.ingramcontent.com/pod-product-compliance
Lightning Source LLC
Chambersburg PA
CBHW081200130726
47996CB00009B/3196